EXPLORING
CAREERS

Careers in Medicine

Leanne Currie-McGhee

ReferencePoint
Press®

For more information, contact:
ReferencePoint Press, Inc.
PO Box 27779
San Diego, CA 92198
www.ReferencePointPress.com

LIBRARY OF CONGRESS CATALOGING-IN-PUBLICATION DATA

Names: Currie-McGhee, L. K. (Leanne K.) author.
Title: Careers in medicine / by Leanne Currie-McGhee.
Description: San Diego, CA : ReferencePoint Press, Inc., 2018. | Series: Exploring careers series | Audience: Grade 9 to 12. | Includes bibliographical references and index.
Identifiers: LCCN 2016055260 (print) | LCCN 2017001453 (ebook) | ISBN 9781682822005 (hardback) | ISBN 9781682822012 (eBook)
Subjects: LCSH: Medicine--Vocational guidance--Juvenile literature. | Medicine--Specialties and specialists--Juvenile literature.
Classification: LCC R690 .C87 2018 (print) | LCC R690 (ebook) | DDC 610.69--dc23
LC record available at https://lccn.loc.gov/2016055260

Contents

A Growing Need

For those who are interested in science and enjoy personal interaction, a career in the medical field provides both of these. Jobs in medicine are also stable, and salaries are above average. From doctors to dietitians, career opportunities in all areas of health care are growing at a much faster pace than the national average for career growth. Specifically, the Bureau of Labor Statistics (BLS) projects an average increase of 19 percent across all medical fields from 2014 to 2024, which is much greater than the average for all occupations. This projection would create about 2.3 million new jobs in the United States over that time. Those who are able to combine people skills with an interest in technology are a good fit for careers in medicine.

Always Needed

Choosing a career in the medical field is a stable choice, as people will always need health care. Even during the most recent period of recession—the so-called Great Recession of 2007–2009—health care employment continued to rise. "Healthcare is recession-proof," wrote Kim Brummett, a senior director at the American Association for Homecare in a spring 2014 BLS newsletter. "There is always a need."

The number of medical professionals is also increasing as more people use the health care system. Two major reasons for this are the growth of the general population in the United States and the expansion of America's elderly population. The Pew Research Center projects that the nation's population will rise to 438 million in 2050—up from 320 million in 2015—and these people will require health care services. Additionally, the number of people aged sixty-five and older is projected to grow by about 40 percent between 2012 and 2022. Generally, the elderly population requires more health care than younger age groups. As a result, the health care industry is expected to add jobs to serve the needs of this expanding population of older Americans.

Another factor in the growing need for medical occupations is the increased number of Americans who obtained health insurance as a result of the 2010 Patient Protection and Affordable Care Act. Even with possible changes in the law, several million more people will continue to have health insurance than before it existed. This will add to the ongoing need for more health care workers.

Higher Salaries

In addition to job stability, choosing to work in a medical-related field often leads to higher-than-average salaries. According to a 2016 article on medical careers in *Forbes* magazine, "While many of the new jobs created since the Great Recession are low-paying retail and restaurant positions with no benefits and little chance of advancement, the growing health care sector offers career paths that lead to generous compensation and a secure future." Specifically, those in the health care industry who worked as practitioners with technical backgrounds (such as registered nurses, physicians and surgeons, and dental hygienists) made, on average, $62,610 annually, as of May 2015. This is much higher than the median annual salary of $36,200 for all occupations in the United States.

Medical careers typically offer higher pay through advancement, and in nearly all health care fields, there are opportunities to take on greater responsibilities. Typically, lower ranks in the profession can rise to become supervisors or managers who oversee the duties of a staff. Other advancement options include specializing in an area, such as becoming an occupational therapist with a pediatric specialization, and providing a particular service.

Educational and Technological Interests

Medical-related fields offer a wide range of jobs that require different levels of education and a variety of skills. Nearly all medical jobs require at least a high school diploma and the completion of a training program that focuses on teaching specific skills needed for the job. For example, licensed practical nurses must attend a one-year LPN

Careers in Medicine

Occupation	Entry-Level Education	2015 Median Pay
Dentist	Doctoral or professional degree	$158,310
Dietitian and nutritionist	Bachelor's degree	$57,910
EMT and paramedic	Postsecondary non-degree award	$31,980
Genetic counselor	Master's degree	$72,090
Licensed practical and licensed vocational nurse	Postsecondary non-degree award	$43,170
Nurse anesthetists, nurse midwife, nurse practitioner	Master's degree	$104,740
Occupational therapist	Master's degree	$80,150
Pharmacist	Doctoral or professional degree	$121,500
Physician assistant	Master's degree	$98,180
Physician and surgeon	Doctoral or professional degree	$187,200
Radiologic and MRI technician	Associate's degree	$58,120
Registered nurse	Bachelor's degree	$67,490

Source: Bureau of Labor Statistics, *Occupational Outlook Handbook*, 2015. www.bls.gov.

program. Other jobs, such as medical resonance imaging (MRI) technologist, require an associate's degree in addition to completing a specialized training program. Master's degrees are required for jobs such as occupational therapists, while doctors, pharmacists, chiropractors, and dentists must complete four-year programs in their respective areas after obtaining a bachelor's degree.

An interest and aptitude for technology is required because the technology used by people in these careers is constantly evolving. Every day, the medical field is changing as new discoveries take hold. For example, those working in the field of MRI technology recently began to implement ViosWorks. This is a new MRI-scanning technology that takes images of the human heart and displays them in seven dimensions: three in space, one in time, and three in velocity, giving a full picture of the heart. The nursing field also regularly makes new advances in patient care. One of the latest is the Drip Clip, a device that automatically calculates an IV infusion drip rate, notes the total volume of the infusion, and can set an alarm to alert a nurse when the drip rate changes or stops. Chiropractors also see developments in their field; an example is the advanced Multiwave Lock System (MLS) laser therapy, which uses a laser to treat pain and inflammation. Nearly all medical-related fields offer an opportunity to work with the latest technology.

For those who want to work with the latest technology, help others, and make a difference in people's lives, the medical field provides this opportunity. Those in this field can help patients prevent disease, treat patients' illnesses and injuries, and help patients function when disabled by a medical issue. Those who have an interest in science, a love of learning, and an enjoyment of people will likely find interesting choices among these career paths, as health care is a growing and varied field.

Chiropractor

A chiropractor's mission is to help patients maintain the health and efficient movement of their joints, muscles, and limbs. Chiropractors do not use drugs or surgery to treat problems in these areas. Instead, they focus on natural remedies, in addition to diet and exercise suggestions, to help their patients. Chiropractors help alleviate patients' neuromuscular pains and aches by making physical adjustments to a patient's spine, neck, and back; specifically, chiropractors use their hands to move and manipulate these areas of their patients with the intent of applying pressure to the affected areas to help alleviate the pain. In addition to manual manipulation, chiropractors use other treatments—such as heat and aquatic-based massage therapy, electric currents, and acupuncture—on the spine, neck, and back, to alleviate any pain the patient is enduring.

Most chiropractors work either in a self-owned practice or in a collective practice with colleagues. Much of the workday consists of reviewing X-rays and other test results, going over

At a Glance
Chiropractor

Minimum Educational Requirements
Doctor of chiropractic (DC) degree

Personal Qualities
Intuitive; attentive; physically strong

Certification and Licensing
State license required

Working Conditions
Indoors, in an office

Salary Range
As of 2015, the median salary was $64,440

Number of Jobs
As of 2014, about 45,200

Future Job Outlook
An increase of 17 percent through 2024

patients' files, and meeting directly with scheduled patients. During an appointment, chiropractors listen to a patient's problems, which may range from lower back pain to migraines. These doctors take X-rays if necessary and review their patients' issues and overall health. They may ask about a patient's medical history, as well as any current symptoms. Chiropractors typically perform a physical examination and check for musculoskeletal conditions or misalignments that might be the cause of the patient's complaint. If necessary, chiropractors might order X-rays or other diagnostic imaging procedures, like magnetic resonance imaging, to help with diagnosis and possible treatment.

Treating patients consists of adjusting and realigning the back and other portions of the musculoskeletal system. By using their hands to adjust the spine into proper alignment, chiropractors relieve pain, restore mobility and range of motion, and reduce strain on other joints and muscles. During these treatments, patients lie on a special bed and the chiropractor applies force to the joints or back, and massage to muscles, as the chiropractor sees fit. Spring Aragon is a chiropractor who treats a lot of navy service members at the Branch Health Clinic in Bangor, Washington. She uses her skills to help her patients deal with physical pain that often results from their jobs. "I primarily look at neck and back issues. That's what we treat about 80 percent of the time. People come in with back pain and that's something they will deal with more than once in their lifetime," said Aragon in a 2015 online article on the US Navy's website. "A lot of patients come in because of the gear they wear, standing for prolonged periods of time, or standing and sitting in static positions which cause a lot of symptoms." Because chiropractic care takes a holistic, or whole-person, approach to a patient's health, chiropractors may also provide advice to promote better health. This advice may include a change in diet and physical activity or specifically recommended exercises.

After seeing their schedule of patients, chiropractors often spend part of their day responding to e-mail or phone inquiries, following up with patients, and reviewing any additional paperwork or test results. They may also research ways to treat a patient or consult with another chiropractor about a difficult diagnosis. At the end of the day, many chiropractors feel satisfied that they have helped people. "In general, the reward of seeing a patient experience improved quality of life is worth all the difficulty in becoming a chiropractor," said Shawn Allen of the Joint Chiropractic in a 2016 article for Doctorly.org. "If you can help reduce or eliminate someone's pain, or help patients lead a healthier and more active lifestyle overall, there's a lot of satisfaction in that."

How Do You Become a Chiropractor?

Education

To become a chiropractor, students must have completed at least ninety semester hours of undergraduate education, with courses in sciences (such as physics, chemistry, and biology) before pursuing a doctor of chiropractic (DC) degree. This is a postgraduate degree that typically takes four years to complete. Across the nation, as of 2014, there were fifteen programs accredited by the Council on Chiropractic Education that offered chiropractic degrees.

Once in a chiropractic program, students take classes in anatomy, physiology, and biology. Additionally, students receive clinical experience, in which they work with patients while supervised by licensed chiropractors. Their clinical experience includes providing patients with spinal assessments, learning spinal adjustment techniques, and offering diagnoses. The American Chiropractic Association states that the average curriculum includes at least forty-two hundred hours of classroom, laboratory, and clinical experience.

Some chiropractors choose to continue their education by training in specialty areas, such as orthopedics and pediatrics, and they receive this training at chiropractic colleges. Other chiropractors may choose to obtain a master's degree in nutrition or sports rehabilitation, allowing them to provide these specialties in their practices. For those who want to either be a partner in a practice or own their own practice, additional business and finance classes can be helpful.

Certification and Licensing

To practice in the United States, chiropractors must obtain a state license. All licenses require that an applicant complete an accredited DC program. Some states require chiropractors to have a bachelor's degree, but others will accept the DC as sufficient education if the person entered a program with at least ninety credit hours of undergraduate education. In addition, all applicants must pass the National Board of Chiropractic Examiners exam, which includes testing on basic sciences, clinical subjects, case studies, and X-ray interpretation and analysis. Some states also require applicants to pass state-specific law exams, called jurisprudence exams, which test applicants on state laws and rules regarding their work. All states require continuing education—a certain amount of approved course work that varies by state—in order to maintain a chiropractic license.

Volunteer Work and Internships

Schools accepting chiropractic students like to see applicants who have volunteered in health care fields. For example, some applicants might have volunteered as an aide at a hospital or nursing home. This volunteer work allows prospective students to be exposed to health care settings and interact with patients. Chiropractic schools look favorably on prospective students who have shown such initiative. Indeed, part of their education will include becoming more accustomed to the hands-on work of medical professionals, and during part of their last two years of study, students will intern for a licensed chiropractor to gain on-the-job experience.

Skills and Personality

Because chiropractors deal directly with patients and their bodies, interpersonal skills are required. During treatment, chiropractors must help their patients remain comfortable and relaxed. Additionally, they need to listen as patients explain their problems, and chiropractors need to have good communication skills as they explain disorders and treatments. Often, their patients are regulars, and chiropractors get to know them well.

Another helpful personality trait is intuitiveness. Chiropractors should be able to take in information given by patients and properly diagnose aches and pains. They need to combine their knowledge of the neuromuscular system and its effects on different parts of the body with their understanding of their patients and their medical complaints.

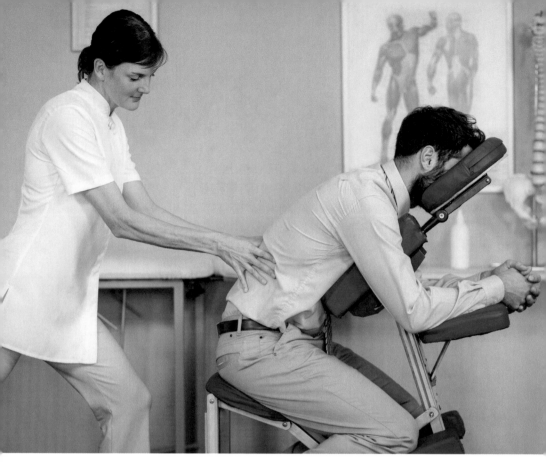

A chiropractor applies pressure and makes minor alignment adjustments to help alleviate a patient's back pain. Neck and back issues represent the bulk of problems chiropractors address.

Because chiropractors use their hands to treat their patients, they should be physically flexible and strong to provide treatment. A chiropractor uses his or her hands to feel the problem and manipulate the appropriate muscles or bones to remedy it. Besides requiring strength to work on patients—at times using force when massaging or manipulating—chiropractors are often on their feet for much of the day. These activities can be physically exhausting, so chiropractors should have the stamina to meet the needs of their patients.

Chiropractors also have a love of learning. Not only do chiropractors require years of education to get into their field, they must also stay current with research and updated techniques as long as they practice their profession. Making sure they are up to date in their treatment methods means they will be better able to respond to the needs of their patients.

On the Job

Employers

Some chiropractors work alongside colleagues in their field in hospitals or clinics. Others own their own practices. For Robert Hayden, who was originally a critical care nurse, one of the reasons he returned to school to become a chiropractor was so that he could start his own practice. "I wanted to create my own little microcosm of health care that was holistic, patient-centered and user-friendly, and I knew that I couldn't do that anywhere other than private practice," Hayden explained in a 2016 online article from *U.S. News & World Report*.

Working Conditions

Chiropractors work in offices, seeing patients throughout the day. They typically work nine-to-five hours, and one out of four works only part time. Some see patients on weekends and after hours. Chiropractors are on their feet much of their day, and they use their bodies, hands, and strength to treat their patients, so the work can be physically demanding and tiring.

Earnings

According to the Bureau of Labor Statistics (BLS), the average salary of chiropractors was $78,370 in 2015. Of these, the lowest 10 percent earned less than $31,310, and the highest 10 percent earned more than $140,580. Geography plays a part in salary; for example, chiropractors in states like California and New York, with more urban areas, earned higher salaries than average, while chiropractors in Texas earned lower-than-average salaries. Additionally, experience plays a part in salary levels. Chiropractors typically earn significantly less early in their careers; they start to earn more as they build up their client rosters and become owners of, or partners in, a practice.

Opportunities for Advancement

Like others who work in self-owned businesses, chiropractors in private practice have no room to advance. For those who work with colleagues in a collective practice, one way to advance is to become a partner within the practice where they work. Additionally, within some clinics, chiropractors can advance to a management position in which they oversee staff. Some chiropractors choose to teach at chiropractic schools and can advance to department heads within their colleges.

What Is the Future Outlook for Chiropractors?

Chiropractors are involved in the growing medical field. According to the BLS, between 2014 and 2024, the employment of chiropractors is projected to grow 17 percent, a much faster growth rate than the average for all occupations. As more people become interested in alternative health care, or health care that complements traditional care, they are turning to chiropractors. Chiropractors appeal to many people because they do not use drugs or surgical methods in their practices. This is reassuring to patients who fear being overmedicated or who believe less invasive methods of healing are a good option. Additionally, according to research company IBISWorld, close to 40 percent of chiropractic patients in the United States are age fifty or above, and as this older population grows, so will the need for chiropractors. These factors seem to support the projection that the nation will need more chiropractors in the coming decade.

Find Out More

American Chiropractic Association (ACA)
1701 Clarendon Blvd., Suite 200
Arlington, VA 22209
website: www.acatoday.org

The ACA is the largest professional association of licensed chiropractors in the United States. It lobbies the government for pro-chiropractic legislation and provides professional and educational opportunities for chiropractors. On its website are key facts and statistics about chiropractors, as well as *ACA Connects*, an online newsletter.

Association of Chiropractic Colleges (ACC)
4424 Montgomery Ave., #202
Bethesda, MD 20814
website: www.chirocolleges.org

The ACC is an association of accredited chiropractic colleges in the United States and affiliate organizations worldwide. Its purpose is to advance chiropractic education, research, and service. The website provides links to member colleges for prospective students to research, as well as general information about what chiropractic practice entails.

Council on Chiropractic Education (CCE)
8049 N. Eighty-Fifth Way
Scottsdale, AZ 85258

The CCE is the national accrediting body for doctor of chiropractic programs at institutions of higher education in the United States. The website maintains an updated list of which institutions offer accredited programs. In addition, the CCE accreditation standards, policies, bylaws, and manuals are accessible from the website.

International Chiropractors Association (ICA)
6400 Arlington Blvd., Suite 800
Falls Church, VA 22042
website: www.chiropractic.org

This organization is the world's oldest international chiropractic professional organization representing practicing chiropractors, students, chiropractic assistants, and educators throughout the world. The ICA works to grow and develop the chiropractic profession, and its website provides links to information for chiropractors, students, and patients.

Dentist

What Does a Dentist Do?

A dentist ensures that people can smile, eat, speak, and drink without problems or pain. A dentist's job includes diagnosing and treating problems of teeth, gums, and related parts of the mouth. Dentists also instruct patients on the best ways to care for their teeth and maintain good oral hygiene. They work with several different types of technology—including X-rays, digital scanners, forceps, and more—to accomplish these tasks.

Most dentists spend the majority of their workday seeing patients. The work dentists complete on patients is often quite technical, involving tools, such as drills and scrapers used to correct issues within the mouth. For regular checkups, dentists will inspect patients' teeth and gums using probes and mirrors to analyze their overall dental health. Dentists usually examine X-rays of the gums, jaws, and teeth to help determine if a patient has any problems in these areas. To resolve problems, dentists perform procedures, such as removing decay from teeth, filling cavities, repairing cracked or fractured teeth, placing sealants on teeth, completing root canals, placing crowns on teeth, and measuring a patient's mouth and teeth for any necessary dental appliances. Additionally, they administer anesthetics to patients to keep pain at bay during some procedures. Dentists find satisfaction in providing their patients with a healthy mouth and smile. "When I do cosmetic work on a patient who was insecure and never smiling and we fixed their teeth and they are very happy with the outcome, that is very satisfying," said Alyssa Veneruso Feinman, a dentist interviewed in a 2015 CNN article.

Most dentists work in private practices. While they spend much of their days working on patients, they also perform other tasks to keep their office running efficiently. For example, they often supervise a staff of dental hygienists who do the bulk of preventive care on patients. This frees the dentists up to do the more exacting surgical

A dentist examines work done on a young patient's teeth. The typical dentist does a variety of procedures, including filling cavities, repairing cracked or fractured teeth, placing sealants or crowns on teeth, and doing root canals.

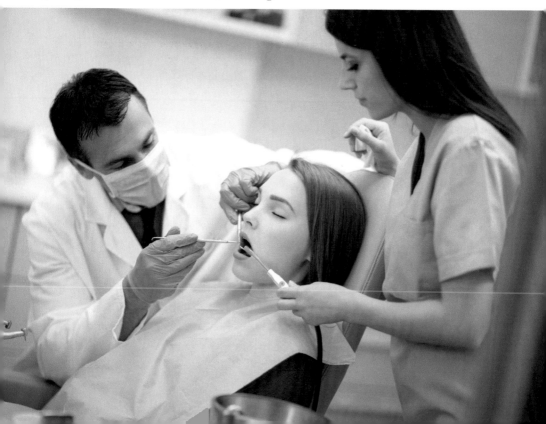

procedures that involve drilling, filling, and straightening teeth. In addition to working with patients, dentists must do routine chores, such as meeting with vendors to purchase supplies, marketing the practice to gain more clients, and handling some administrative duties. Dentists often employ a staff to schedule and bill patients, but it is the dentists who must ensure that their employees are paid, insurance practices are followed, and accounting is kept up to date. "I am surprised how much of my daily job isn't performing dental treatment and how much of my work follows me home at night," states Ryan Dulde, a dentist who owns his own practice, in an interview on the American Student Dental Association website. Dulde finds himself reviewing budgets, placing orders, and overseeing marketing in addition to seeing his patients.

No matter what career path a dentist chooses, he or she will likely spend part of the day working with patients and the rest of the day completing administrative tasks. Most dentists are generally satisfied with these duties and their jobs overall. In fact, *U.S. News & World Report* ranked dentist as the best job in the United States in 2015. This decision was based on predictions by the Bureau of Labor Statistics (BLS) on job growth, salary prospects, and overall job satisfaction.

How Do You Become a Dentist?

Education

According to the American Dental Association (ADA), students interested in pursuing dental careers would help their chances by taking higher-level science and math classes while in high school. Most dental schools require a bachelor's degree for admission and the completion of certain undergraduate courses, such as biology, physics, and chemistry. A major in biology or another science will increase a student's chances of being accepted to dental school. Additionally, dentists recommend that applicants work on their dexterity by painting, drawing, or doing an exacting type of work to prepare them for dentistry.

In 2015, there were more than sixty dental schools accredited in the United States by the Commission on Dental Accreditation, which is part of the ADA. To apply to these schools, applicants must take the Dental Admission Test during their junior year of college. The competition to enter a dental school can be high, so a good score on this test—along with a high grade point average and a successful interview with the school—are assets when applying.

Once in dental school, the first two years are spent in the class-room and laboratory, learning about basic health sciences, such as anatomy, biochemistry, and microbiology. Additionally, students learn the principles of oral diagnosis and treatment, and they may practice their skills on mannequins and models. Some programs have students begin treating actual patients toward the end of the second year. During the third and fourth years of dental school, students will be treating patients under the supervision of licensed dental faculty.

While treating patients, student dentists generally complete common procedures, such as teeth cleaning and fillings; they do not do specialized work. Most will be assigned to practice their skills in community clinics, outpatient clinics, and hospitals. Michael Saba remembers the favorite part of his last year at dental school was us-ing his skills to help a woman who had lost some of her teeth and was without hope of restoring them. In a 2014 interview posted on the American Student Dental Association website, Saba discussed how he fitted this patient with dentures. Saba said, "My favorite part of the past school year was delivering dentures to a hopeless case. The smile on my patient's face was so big that I thought her teeth were going to fall out."

During the final year of dental school, students take management courses in order to learn effective communication skills and business operations. This is because most dentists either end up owning their own businesses or working in a collective dental office setting. In ei-ther case, they must become familiar with the business aspect of the profession.

In the United States, a graduate of dental school is awarded the DDS, doctor of dental surgery degree, or the DMD, doctor of dental medicine degree, depending on the type of dental school attended. (The degrees are actually the same, with the same curriculum.) Af-ter completing their four-year degree, dentists choose either to go into general practice or to specialize in one of nine areas, such as periodontics or pediatric dentistry. If they choose to specialize, they will continue education in one of these areas. To specialize in these areas, students need to complete a two-year residency program after finishing dental school.

Certification and Licensing

All states require a dental license to practice. To obtain a license, candidates must graduate from a US dental school accredited by the ADA and pass Parts I and II of the written National Board Dental Examinations. These exams are made up of multiple-choice questions. Part I is a comprehensive examination covering the basic biomedical sciences, dental anatomy, and ethics, while Part II is a comprehensive examination that covers clinical dental subjects, including patient management. Additionally, most US licensing jurisdictions require candidates to take a clinical examination. Each state establishes its own clinical examination requirement, and most state boards of dentistry rely on a regional testing agency to administer the examination.

Volunteer Work and Internships

High school students interested in dental careers can learn more about them by volunteering. The ADA recommends volunteering at a local dentist's, orthodontist's, or pediatric dentist's office. If a student cannot find a local office that takes volunteers, the ADA recommends contacting the nearest dental society (which can be done through the ADA website).

Skills and Personality

Extreme attention to detail and precision are necessary skills for dentists. Much of their work follows specific procedures and must be completed precisely to ensure success. For example, a dentist needs precision to match the color of a crown or an implanted tooth with a person's natural teeth. A dentist must understand how to perform step-by-step technical procedures and what to do when encountering any issues outside of the norm.

Because they work in the mouth, dentists must be dexterous with their hands as they handle various tools in small spaces. A dentist needs to combine manual dexterity with good coordination because of the movements required during intricate procedures. Any mistake could cause permanent damage to a person's teeth or mouth.

Richard J. Reinitz, who has worked as a dentist for more than twenty-five years, believes that being a caring person is also essential to being a good dentist. He feels that a dentist's relationship with his or her patients is extremely important, as a dentist needs to be able to reassure patients and attend to their needs. Reinitz wrote in a 2016 Dental Economics online article, "Treatment of a patient is not limited to mechanical diagnosis and treatment. A patient must believe that the person caring for him or her is not only knowledgeable but cares whether the patient gets better or not." Reinitz calls his surgical and root canal patients the day after a procedure to check in with them. He believes patients need to know that their dentist cares about them and is interested in their well-being.

On the Job

Employers

According to the BLS, in 2014 one out of four dentists was self-employed. The remainder typically work within a collective practice with other dentists. A few who enter the academic field are usually employed by dental schools to teach the next generation of dentists.

Working Conditions

Dentists mainly work in offices. They spend much of the day on their feet treating patients. For physical safety reasons, they wear masks, gloves, and safety glasses to protect themselves from infectious diseases that can be spread through blood or bodily fluids. The majority of dentists work full time during regular work hours. Many dentists are also on call for patients who have dental emergencies during off hours.

Earnings

In 2015, according to the BLS, the average salary for a general dentist was $172,350. Dentists' earnings depend on their location, how many hours they work, and how long they have been in practice. Dentists in wealthier, highly populated areas tend to be paid better than those in rural and poorer regions of the country. For example, the average salary of a dentist in New Hampshire is $227,160, while a dental colleague in Indiana will earn only $146,760 on average.

Opportunities for Advancement

A dentist within a collective practice can advance by becoming a partner in the office. Being a partner provides the benefits of receiving part of the office's profits and part ownership of the practice; along with the benefits of being a partner come responsibilities, such as helping to run the administrative and business side of the office.

What Is the Future Outlook for Dentists?

According to the BLS, the employment of dentists is projected to grow 18 percent from 2014 to 2024. This is much faster than the average for all occupations. There are a few reasons that explain this projection. The percentage of older Americans is growing, and these individuals will require more dental services over their lifetime. Additionally, changes in health care laws have provided more people with medical and dental coverage. And statistically, people who are covered by dental insurance are more likely to visit a dentist, leading to a greater need for these services.

Find Out More

Academy of General Dentistry (AGD)
560 W. Lake St., Sixth Floor
Chicago, IL 60661
website: www.agd.org

The AGD is a professional association of more than forty thousand dentists dedicated to providing quality dental care and oral health education to the public. The website contains information on conferences and webinars that provide education for dentists as well as information for patients on how to care for their teeth and other related issues.

American Dental Association (ADA)
211 E. Chicago Ave.
Chicago, IL 60611
website: www.ada.org

The ADA is the nation's largest dental association and represents more than 159,000 dentist members. It provides oral health–related information and research for dentists and their patients. The website offers information on dental careers and the path to attain them.

American Dental Education Association (ADEA)
655 K St. NW, Suite 800
Washington, DC 20001
website: www.adea.org

The ADEA is composed of corporations, programs, and more than twenty thousand individuals. The ADEA's activities include research, advocacy, and communications about dental issues. Its website provides information on how dentists can continue their education, as well as keep up with the latest dental developments and career opportunities.

American Student Dental Association (ASDA)
211 E. Chicago Ave., Suite 700
Chicago, IL 60611
website: www.asdanet.org

The ASDA is a national student-run organization that protects and advances the rights, interests, and welfare of dental students. The ASDA website provides students interested in dental school with information regarding application, prerequisites, and student loans. It also has interviews with dental students and dentists about their work and daily tasks.

Dietitian

What Does a Dietitian Do?

A person who is interested in helping people obtain or maintain good health through nutrition may want to consider becoming a dietitian. A dietitian is an expert in making food choices that help people maintain health or deal with symptoms of a medical condition. A dietitian works closely with clients to develop nutrition programs for them or to develop menus for an entire group of people, such as at a school. Dietitians can work in a variety of settings: at a clinic, hospital, community program, health club, or food service department of a large factory or other facility. Some work for themselves, taking on clients who consult them directly.

Dietitians who work in settings such as clinics and hospitals are called clinical dietitians. Their duties include creating nutritional programs based on the health needs of patients or residents, and they counsel patients on how nutrition can lead to a healthier lifestyle. They coordinate medical records, information from nurses and doctors, and nutritional needs to make

At a Glance

Dietitian

Minimum Educational Requirements

Bachelor's degree

Personal Qualities

Analytical; personable; detailed

Certification and Licensing

State license required; Registered Dietitian Nutritionist certification optional

Working Conditions

Indoors, in office or visiting homes

Salary Range

As of 2015, the median salary was $57,910

Number of Jobs

As of 2015, about 66,700

Future Job Outlook

An increase of 16 percent through 2024

individual plans based on their findings. Their role often involves adjusting the person's intake of vitamins, fluids, nutrients, or calories. For example, they ensure that sodium-restricted diets are in place for those with high blood pressure or liver disease, or they develop a protein-restrictive diet for those suffering from kidney disease.

Margaret Farnsworth, senior clinical dietitian at the Methodist Hospital in Houston, Texas, explains that the dietitians she supervises spend their days seeing patients, reviewing patient information, developing plans based on their information, and ensuring these plans are carried out. She says that her dietitians see fifteen to twenty patients a day. They make plans for these patients, check patients' charts to see if anything regarding their health has changed, ensure the facility provides the patients their planned meals, and educate the patients on how to follow these plans on their own. "We interact with patients and their (families) to make sure the patient is eating well and understands any diet restrictions they may have while they are in our care, and we try to educate patients and family members to ensure they understand the important role that nutrition plays in the healing process," Farnsworth explained in a 2013 online *Houston Chronicle* article.

Community dietitians are those who work at wellness programs, health organizations, public health agencies, day care centers, health clubs, and recreational camps and resorts, where they develop nutritional programs. Some community dietitians also make home visits to patients who are too physically ill to attend consultation in health facilities. Community dietitians are becoming more prevalent as companies include wellness programs as a paid benefit for their employees. "In 2014, 92% of companies with 200 employees or more had some type of wellness program," says Lindsey Mariano, a health coaching facilitator at Provant, a health and wellness solutions provider for businesses nationwide.

Dietitians can also choose to work in food service settings at hospitals, prisons, and schools, where they are called management dietitians. Their jobs include purchasing food and planning for the meals to be served to groups of people at the facilities. They use their knowledge to provide nutritional choices that meet the variety of dietary needs of the people they serve. Additionally, they must complete business tasks, such as budgeting for their purchases and overseeing kitchen staff.

Another option for a dietitian is to set up his or her own business and work as a consultant. These dietitians work to gain individual clients who seek them out to create personal nutrition plans to help them gain or lose weight, increase energy levels, or deal with medical issues such as diabetes. A job like this can be flexible, as these dietitians can create their own schedule.

All dietitians work in some way with nutrition and developing eating plans for others. The different choices of jobs available to dietitians provide different levels of flexibility and salary. For those who enjoy the satisfaction of working to improve the health of others through nutrition and seeing the effects of their work, this can be a stimulating career.

How Do You Become a Dietitian?

Education

Registered dietitians and nutritionists must first obtain a bachelor's degree in subjects such as food science, nutrition science, or dietetics. These programs include courses in nutrition, psychology, chemistry, and biology. "The Nutrition courses were challenging in my program, but they weren't impossible. The workload was tough, but the actual information wasn't difficult to understand," writes Kath, a registered dietitian, in her blog *Kath Eats Real Food*. Students must attend bachelor's programs that are certified by the Accreditation Council for Education in Nutrition and Dietetics (ACEND). Additionally, some students decide to continue their education and obtain a graduate degree within the field, although this is not a requirement to obtain a license.

After graduating, dietitians and nutritionists then must undergo several hundred hours of supervised training, in the form of a Direct Internship (DI) through an accredited program with colleges, hospitals, and clinics. Students must apply to accredited DI programs online through the Dietetic Internship Centralized Application Service. Additionally, there are some dietetic schools that offer coordinated programs that allow students to complete supervised training as part of their undergraduate or graduate course work. During their training, dietetic students learn how to determine a person's specific nutritional needs based on their health and physical status, and how to meet these nutritional needs.

Certification and Licensing

A majority of states require dietitians and nutritionists to obtain licenses in order to practice. Those that require a state license usually require that dietitians possess a bachelor's degree in food and nutrition or a related area, complete supervised practice, such as an internship, and pass an exam. Four states do not require dietitians to be licensed. Some only require a state registration or certification to practice as a dietitian, and a few states have no regulations at all for this occupation.

Many dietitians choose to earn the registered dietitian nutritionist (RDN) title. This is not a required title to work as a dietitian, but often the requirements to obtain a state license are the same as those needed to obtain an RDN title, so many dietitians choose to obtain both. Some companies and health facilities that hire dietitians prefer that candidates have the RDN.

To receive an RDN, dietitians and nutritionists must, at minimum, have a bachelor's degree and, after completing the degree, complete a DI accredited with ACEND. Additionally, dietitians who want the RDN must pass a national examination administered by the Commission on Dietetic Registration. In order to maintain the RDN, dietitians and nutritionists must complete seventy-five continuing professional education credits every five years.

Volunteer Work and Internships

All licensed dietitians must complete their internship, a DI, which is not an easy task. Obtaining a DI is challenging because of the competition to get these appointments. Becoming involved in undergraduate nutrition clubs that do volunteer work, such as visiting elementary schools and teaching about nutrition, will help boost a student's credentials when applying for a DI. "Being a member of your campus nutrition club is the easiest way to get involved and make a name for yourself in your program. Volunteer, join a committee, or even run for office! While in undergrad, I served as my student dietetic association's newsletter editor and was also active in committees," wrote Kristina Todini, a registered dietitian, in a 2015 entry on her *Fork in the Road* blog.

Skills and Personality

Being personable is necessary for dietitians because often their day involves meeting and interacting with patients or clients. They need to be able to listen to their clients' wants and needs and help them accept any necessary nutrition changes for their health. Interacting well with a client helps build a trusting relationship that will benefit the patient and dietitian.

The work of dietitians includes a lot of analysis. They must be able to interpret the latest scientific studies and nutrition science when developing food plans. They need to assess a client's overall health and understand his or her personal dietary needs. Dietitians take in a variety of factors, such as the client's age, physical activity, and work life, when determining an overall nutrition menu for them.

Technical skills are also necessary because dietitians work with health-related tools and equipment, including calorimeters to gauge metabolism, glucose meters to evaluate blood sugar, and bioelectric impedance machines to electronically measure body fat. They need technical training to use these devices accurately. They also need some computer skills to use medical software, as well as the latest computer programs, to create printed plans for clients.

On the Job

Employers

Thirty percent of dietitians work at state, private, and local hospitals as clinical dietitians. Management dietitians work in food settings within schools, prisons, and other facilities. Wellness companies, fitness facilities, and companies with wellness programs also hire community dietitians. Additionally, 11 percent of dietitians are self-employed, developing their own businesses to provide clients with nutritional advice.

Working Conditions

Most dietitians and nutritionists work full time, but about one out of four works part time. Dietitians may work evenings and weekends to meet with clients who are unavailable at other times. Some work within a facility, visiting patients each day, while others work in an office, ordering and planning meals for an institution, and still others may visit clients at their homes, educating them on their meal plans.

Earnings

According to the Academy of Nutrition and Dietetics, the average annual salary for a dietitian is $63,700. This varies depending on the dietitian's experience, job location, and responsibilities. According to the Mayo Clinic, salary increases as experience increases, and many registered dietitians—particularly those in management, business, and consulting—earn incomes of $75,000 to $92,700 per year.

Opportunities for Advancement

A clinical dietitian has an opportunity to advance by becoming a manager of other dietitians or by becoming the coordinator of a program within the facility. Those working in food service also have an opportunity to advance into management positions where they can oversee a department and gain higher salaries as a result.

What Is the Future Outlook for Dietitians?

The Bureau of Labor Statistics projects that this field's employment will increase 16 percent through 2024, which is much faster than the average for all occupations. One of the reasons for this is that more medical insurance providers are covering client visits with dietitians. Additionally, with the increasing number of obese and overweight Americans, the popularity of weight-management programs has grown, leading to a need for more dietitians. Also, because of increasing obesity there is a higher population of people dealing with diabetes, resulting in a greater need in the community for diabetic education programs requiring nutritional health care.

Find Out More

Academy of Nutrition and Dietetics
120 S. Riverside Plaza, Suite 2000
Chicago, IL 60606
website: www.eatrightpro.org

This organization and its website provide information on how to become an RDN, as well as professional development possibilities after becoming one. It also provides the latest information on health advocacy issues with which the organization is involved. Additionally, the website provides information to help dietitians improve their practice in the field.

International Confederation of Dietetic Associations (ICDA)
480 University Ave., Suite 604
Toronto, Ontario M5G 1V2
Canada
website: www.internationaldietetics.org

The ICDA represents about 160,000 dietitians and nutritionists around the world. The ICDA supports national dietetics associations and their members by providing guidance and standards of education and training for the profession. Additionally, it promotes the role of nutrition and dietetics professionals in enhancing health and reducing disease.

School Nutrition Association
120 Waterfront St., Suite 300
National Harbor, MD 20745
website: https://schoolnutrition.org

This national organization is committed to advancing the quality of school meal programs through education and advocacy. It strives to see that all children have access to healthful school meals and nutrition education. Its website provides information on how to develop school nutrition plans, how to obtain certificates in school nutrition, and newsletters.

Today's Dietitian
3801 Schuylkill Rd.
Spring City, PA 19475
website: www.todaysdietitian.com

Today's Dietitian is an online resource for nutrition professionals providing the latest nutrition information and research. The website provides information on how nutrition can help ease a variety of health issues from allergies and diabetes. A wide variety of topics from weight control to nutritional needs by age are on the website.

Licensed Practical Nurse

What Does a Licensed Practical Nurse Do?

At a Glance

Licensed Practical Nurse

Minimum Educational Requirements

High school diploma or GED

Personal Qualities

Empathetic; physically fit; patient

Certification and Licensing

Certification and state license required

Working Conditions

Indoors, in office or visiting homes

Salary Range

As of 2015, the median pay was $43,170

Number of Jobs

As of 2015, about 719,900

Future Job Outlook

An increase of 16 percent through 2024

Licensed practical nurses (LPNs) spend their days providing basic nursing care to patients. They help their patients complete daily tasks, such as bathing, dressing, eating, and using the bathroom. They also perform some medical duties, such as checking blood pressure, dressing a patient's wounds, or helping ensure that patients take the correct dosage of their medications. They even treat bedsores, prepare and give injections and enemas, give alcohol rubs and massages, apply ice packs and hot water bottles, and monitor catheters. LPNs can be found in a variety of medical settings, and their specific duties depend upon the setting in which they work.

Many LPNs are employed by hospitals where they normally work under the supervision of a registered nurse (RN). Registered nurses attend school longer than LPNs do and are authorized to take on more responsibilities than LPNs. In a hospital, the main duties of LPNs include taking patients' vital signs and cleaning up and dressing injuries. Additionally, some hospitalized patients might need help during physical therapy, and LPNs are there to help turn patients over, assist them in getting out of bed, and perform other exercises that require patients to be repositioned. In hospitals, LPNs often record vital data on patient charts for doctor and RN review. These charts are extremely important tools that communicate vital information about patients. Charting duties involve taking down vital signs, listing procedures, making notes, and writing down billing codes.

LPNs who work in nursing homes are more involved in assisting patients with daily tasks. Under the supervision of the head RN, LPNs are responsible for the patient's bathing, eating, and daily hygiene, such as teeth brushing. Other daily tasks include getting the patient out of bed, moving the patient into a more comfortable position, and helping the patient to the dining room or other areas. As in hospitals, these LPNs take and record the vital signs of patients. Additionally, LPNs in nursing homes may need to provide medical assistance, such as applying bandages and dressings, inserting catheters, and monitoring IVs. They are there to ensure that the patients are comfortable and that basic medical needs are attended to.

Physicians' offices are another place where LPNs can find work. In physicians' offices, LPNs may work either on the patient care or administrative side of the office. "[A] great bonus to working in a physician's office is that there are usually two routes that you can pursue," writes Emily Belcher, an LPN, on PracticalNursing.org. "On one route, you can work in the clinical area. Some of your job duties will be taking vital signs, administering medications and/or shots, performing EKG's, pulmonary function tests (PFT's). . . . The second route is administrative. You can work behind the scenes and answer calls, take messages for the doctor, call patients." She adds that some LPNs can take on both duties.

LPNs may also choose to work as home health aides, which allows them to travel to patients throughout the day. These LPNs provide both basic nursing care and assistance with daily tasks to patients in their homes. Their typical patients include children with chronic illnesses or developmental problems, and seniors with mild to moderate health issues. Their visits allow their patients to remain at home while still having their basic medical needs met.

No matter where an LPN works, his or her main responsibility is the patient's health. People with an interest in helping others directly will find this to be a rewarding career. Although the salary is on the lower end of the scale—as it requires less formal education than higher-paid medical careers—it is a steady job with many prospects. An LPN is in the position to comfort people and help them through difficult times, providing a meaningful career.

How Do You Become a Licensed Practical Nurse?

Education

In order to become a licensed practical nurse, individuals first must graduate from high school or obtain their GED before applying to an accredited LPN program. Each state has accredited LPN programs offered at various institutions. Admission to these programs varies by state; in addition to a high school diploma or GED, some programs require that applicants pass an entrance exam prior to acceptance.

Normally, these programs award a certificate or diploma, and take about a year to a year and a half to complete. The majority of these programs are offered at technical schools and community colleges, but some programs are also available in high school vocational programs or within hospitals. Students in these programs combine classroom learning, in which they take subjects such as nursing, biology, and pharmacology, with clinical experience that includes learning how to take vital signs and attending to minor medical needs of patients.

Certification and Licensing

States require that LPNs obtain a license in order to practice. Students must complete LPN programs to receive certification, and then they must pass the National Council Licensure Examination for Practical Nurses (NCLEX-PN) to obtain a state license. The NCLEX test for practical nurses is computerized and includes approximately 85 to 205 test items to be completed within five hours. According to the National Council of State Boards of Nursing, in 2013 more than 84 percent of first-time takers passed the NCLEX-PN. Additionally, some states require LPNs to complete continuing education to maintain their license; for example, in Florida LPNs must complete twenty-four hours of continuing education classes every two years.

Volunteer Work and Internships

Before becoming an LPN, volunteering in a nursing home or other medical facility will help a person determine if this is a good career choice. Volunteer opportunities are available through organizations like the Red Cross or through local facilities, such as nursing homes.

Skills and Personality

As LPNs work closely with patients, empathy is necessary to handle delicate interactions. LPNs often perform duties that require them to help their patients with personal tasks, such as bathing or eating, and medical tasks, such as providing intravenous medication or taking specimens; these tasks can cause a patient discomfort or even embarrassment. LPNs need to be able to put their patients at ease and help comfort them. "If you truly have a heart for service and caring for others, then this career path can be quite rewarding," states the ECPI University blog in the *The Ugly Truth About a Practical Nursing Career*.

Patience is another quality necessary for an LPN. When they are dealing with serious issues and loss of abilities, patients may not always be pleasant or kind to those helping them. "When people are ill, they become scared—so do their families. When people are scared, they tend to lash out. If you are impatient, I feel it makes things a whole lot worse," wrote Sami Aakhus in a 2016 article on PracticalNursing .org. Taking the time to listen to patients describe and discuss their problems will help LPNs more successfully accomplish their tasks.

It is also helpful if an LPN is physically fit. LPNs spend much of their days standing, walking, lifting their patients, and pushing patients' wheelchairs. Additionally, they usually work twelve-hour shifts with few breaks as they are attending to patients. Both endurance and strength will help them complete the duties of their job and see to the needs of their patients.

On the Job

Employers

LPNs typically work alongside colleagues with patients in hospitals, nursing homes, rehabilitation centers, and medical offices. According to the Bureau of Labor Statistics (BLS), in 2014, 38 percent of LPNs worked at nursing and residential care facilities, 17 percent were employed by hospitals, and 13 percent worked in physician offices. Other LPNs work primarily on their own, traveling to see patients at their residences. Specifically, 11 percent worked for home health care companies, providing services to patients in their homes, in 2014.

Working Conditions

Licensed practical nurses work indoors and are often on their feet as they assist patients. Throughout the day, they visit patients either in different locations within a facility such as a hospital, or as they visit different homes for home health care visits. Their work is physically demanding; they often are required to lift and move patients.

Most licensed practical vocational nurses work full time, with only one in five working part time. Many LPNs work nights, weekends, and holidays, because medical care takes place at all hours. Those who work in hospitals and clinics often work twelve-hour shifts.

Being in a medical profession, LPNs come into contact with biological hazards, such as blood and other bodily fluids. They must take precautions by wearing gloves and gowns during any contact with such hazards. Additionally, they deal with needles and other tools, so they must follow safety procedures to not harm themselves.

Earnings

According to the BLS, the average annual salary of LPNs in 2015 was $44,030. An LPN's place of employment affects the level of his or her salary. LPNs who worked at nursing care facilities earned an average salary of $44,500, but those who worked in offices of physicians received an average salary of $40,950. Additionally, LPNs who work in states with prosperous urban environments typically earn more than those in states with more rural areas.

Opportunities for Advancement

LPNs who are looking to advance their career in the medical field typically choose to return to school and obtain their RN or other higher-level medical degree. There are also management and supervisory positions available to LPNs. An LPN may advance to supervise the day-to-day nursing activities of a facility, managing certified nursing assistants and/or other LPNs. In this position, an LPN may assign patient care, train others, and determine schedules.

What Is the Future Outlook for Licensed Practical Nurses?

The BLS projects a 16 percent growth between 2014 and 2024 with an addition of 117,300 LPN jobs. This is higher than the national average for all occupations. Several different factors have led to this projection. For one, several chronic health issues, such as diabetes and obesity, have become more prevalent in recent years and are projected to continue to rise. With more people requiring treatment, this will likely lead to a greater number of LPNs on staff at health facilities and serving as home health aides. Additionally, statistics show that the older population is increasing, suggesting that there will be a growing number of patients at nursing home facilities where LPN services are required. Studies also show that more elderly people are opting to stay in their homes as they age, and it is likely many of these people will require some assistance with daily care. Finally, more medical procedures at hospitals are being done on an outpatient basis, and LPNs are needed to provide home visits for discharged patients, to ensure the patients receive proper care. Brett Casteel, an LPN student at Southeastern Illinois College, explained his reason for entering the program in a 2016 online news article: "I need a job that's going to go and last, so I'm working towards nursing." Indeed, all factors indicate a stable and growing career field for LPNs.

Find Out More

American Association of Nurse Practitioners (AANP)
PO Box 12846
Austin, TX 78711
website: www.aanp.org

This is the largest and only full-service national professional membership organization for nurse practitioners of all specialties. Its purpose is to empower all nurse practitioners to advance health care through practice, education, and research. The website includes information on continuing education and provides online medical journals.

National Association for Practical Nurse Education and Service (NAPNES)
2071 N. Bechtle Ave. PMB 307
Springfield, OH 45504
website: www.napnes.org

The NAPNES is dedicated to promoting the education and regulation of LPNs. This organization is responsible for the legislation that provides for the licensure of LPNs. Its website provides e-training for those in these professions, and an online magazine, *Journal of Practical Nursing*.

National Council of State Boards of Nursing (NCSBN)
111 E. Wacker Dr., Suite 2900
Chicago, IL 60601
website: www.ncsbn.org

The NCSBN is a nonprofit organization dedicated to developing and administering nurse licensure and certification examinations. The exams they develop include the NCLEX-RN and NCLEX-PN examinations, in addition to other nursing exams. The website provides details on the nursing exams, how to prepare, and how to sign up for them.

National Federation of Licensed Practical Nurses (NFLPN)
3801 Lake Boone Trail, Suite 190
Raleigh, NC 27607
website: www.nflpn.org

The NFLPN is a professional organization for licensed practical nurses, licensed vocational nurses, and nursing students in the United States. It provides continuous certification and learning for its members. Its website provides insight on what LPNs do, their current salaries, where they are hired, and how to enter the field.

MRI Technologist

People who love working hands on with the latest technology might find magnetic resonance imaging (MRI) an interesting field. MRI technologists operate MRI scanners that produce strong magnetic fields and radio pulses to create high-definition, three-dimensional pictures of organs and soft tissues inside the body. Soft tissues can be difficult to see due to bones, but MRI images are able to reveal the state of these tissues. For this reason, MRI images are essential diagnostic tools that provide doctors with information needed to make important health decisions. The images are especially helpful for doctors investigating issues with the brain, heart, and muscles. A skilled MRI technologist will produce high-resolution images that allow physicians to diagnose problems with accuracy.

MRI technologists typically work either at a hospital, a physician's office, or an MRI diagnostic center. MRI technologists' duties are similar no matter where they work. They see patients throughout the day, conducting MRI scans requested

At a Glance

MRI Technologist

Minimum Educational Requirements

High school diploma or GED

Personal Qualities

Communicative; compassionate; detail oriented

Certification and Licensing

MRI certification and state license required

Working Conditions

Indoors, in MRI laboratories

Salary Range

As of 2015, the median salary was $68,340

Number of Jobs

As of 2015, about 33,460

Future Job Outlook

An increase of 10 percent through 2024

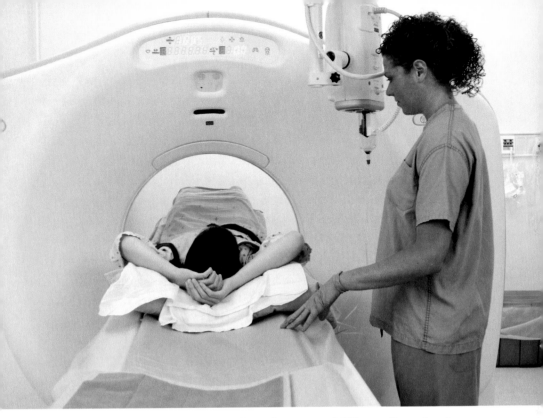

An MRI technologist prepares a patient for undergoing an MRI scan. Operating the scanner, skilled technologists produce high-quality images of organs and soft tissue that a doctor can use to diagnose a health problem.

by physicians. Before meeting with a patient, a technologist reviews the patient's file to understand what area of the patient needs to be scanned. Then the technologist meets with the patient and asks questions to ensure he or she does not have any medical issues that could hinder a scan. For example, a metal plate or a screw in the body could potentially interact with the MRI magnetic field and cause problems with the scan. "MRI Technologists have to wear many hats," Teri Blair, an MRI technologist, said in a 2016 *U.S. News & World Report* online article. "We have to be detectives and screen patients to make sure they can be scanned."

Once he or she determines a patient can be scanned, the technologist prepares the patient for scanning. To ensure an accurate scan is made, the technologist explains the procedure to the patient. Then, the technologist helps position the patient on the scanner and reassures the patient by answering any questions or concerns. Many patients are nervous about undergoing an MRI; the process involves lying inside the MRI machine, which is like a large tube, while the machine emits loud noises. MRI technologists must ensure that patients are calm and able to lie still throughout the procedure. When the patient is situated in the MRI scanner, the MRI technologist calibrates the machine (adjusts it for accuracy), conducts the scan, and records the images for a physician to interpret.

Although much of the job is quite technical, an MRI technologist's job includes much personal interaction. They work closely with their patients, particularly those who are dealing with long-term issues. "I love working in the hospital setting, but it can be stressful," says Devonné Franks, who earned an associate's degree in Applied Sciences in Medical Imaging. "I see patients who are very sick, some with incurable diseases. I always remember those patients as I tend to get to know them over time."

The satisfaction of helping physicians diagnose patient problems provides a satisfying career. Additionally, MRI technologists are in a growing field, and they are able to maintain an above-average salary throughout their career. This job is for those who enjoy a combination of working with highly technical equipment and interacting with many different patients and a team of medical professionals.

How Do You Become an MRI Technologist?

Education

According to the Bureau of Labor Statistics (BLS), high school students who are interested in radiologic or MRI technology should take courses that focus on math and science, such as anatomy, biology, chemistry, physiology, and physics. Additionally, obtaining certification in cardiopulmonary resuscitation is helpful when entering any health field.

After graduating from high school, the most common path for those who aspire to become MRI technologists is to attend an MRI technology certificate program. Several of these are two-year programs, and most programs result in students graduating with an associate's degree and certification, although some only provide certification. When enrolling, a student should make sure the program is accredited by the Joint Review Committee on Education in Radiologic Technology or the Commission on Accreditation of the American Registry of Magnetic Resonance Imaging Technologists.

During these programs, students will study pathology, anatomy, physiology, medical terminology, patient care, MRI equipment safety, and ethics. Additionally, they will receive extensive hands-on training in a variety of clinical settings, working with actual patients and equipment. After graduating and obtaining a certification, newly hired technologists complete a period of on-the-job training during which they follow an experienced mentor through typical workdays.

A second route to this career path is to enter it after first working in another health care field. Many technologists become certified in MRI after having already earned certifications in radiography or similar areas. Since the candidates' previous work and training provided the basic sciences and humanities courses, they do not need to enter a full academic program. Instead, they need to obtain MRI skills through a shorter program and training period, often provided at a hospital. This type of MRI certification takes typically one year or less, and it focuses specifically on the skills and knowledge necessary for magnetic resonance imaging.

Certification and Licensing

Most states mandate that MRI technologists obtain licenses to practice, but the requirements vary. However, most license requirements include graduation from an accredited program and passing a knowledge exam. MRI technologists may opt to obtain national certification through the American Registry of Magnetic Resonance Imaging Technologists, and several states accept this certification in lieu of passing a state test in order to obtain a state license. One way to obtain national certification is to complete an MRI educational program accredited by the American Registry of Radiologic Technologists (ARRT) and pass the ARRT certification and registration examination in magnetic resonance imaging. The other path is reserved for candidates who previously obtained certification in Radiography or Nuclear Medicine Technology; these individuals must verify their certification in that field and document MRI clinical experience to obtain their national certification.

Once certified and licensed, MRI technologists must engage in regular continuing education in order to maintain their credentials. Specifically, registered technologists must complete twenty-four continuing education credits every two years of their career.

Volunteer Work and Internships

Prior to entering an MRI program, volunteering at a hospital or other medical facility will provide an opportunity to discover what it is like to work in a health-related setting. Additionally, volunteering in these types of facilities will allow a person to gain experience in working with patients, which is helpful for technologists.

Skills and Personality

An essential skill for an MRI technologist is the ability to communicate well. MRI technologists must clearly explain procedures to their patients, provide instructions regarding what the patient must do during the procedure, and answer any questions the patients have.

Being compassionate also will help an MRI technologist develop a patient's trust, which is necessary to complete a successful scan. Most MRI machines require that a patient lie in a tube for up to forty minutes while loud noises occur; some patients panic or develop claustrophobia. "Basically we're asking [patients] not to move for 30 minutes to an hour in a strange, scary environment," says Blair. Being calm and understanding will help soothe the patient and enable him or her to lie still for the duration of the scan.

An aptitude for technical work is needed in order to be a successful MRI technologist. MRI machines are among the latest developments in technology, and a person must be able to learn and understand how they work, how to operate them, and how to calibrate them. As technology is always advancing, MRI technologists must be able to understand and adapt to every new development.

MRI technologists must also be detail oriented. The machines they work with are highly technical, requiring calibration and precise settings to create the required image. Technologists must ensure that the machines are operated accurately. Also, an MRI technologist must be detail oriented when preparing a patient for a scan, ensuring all the setup is done completely and accurately, and that all questions have been asked and answered.

On the Job

Employers

Most MRI technologists work full-time schedules in hospitals, outpatient centers, and MRI diagnostic laboratories. Of these, more than half of MRI technicians work in the imaging departments of hospitals. Diagnostic laboratories employ approximately 20 percent of MRI technologists. Physicians' offices are also beginning to employ a growing number of MRI technologists as these offices are adding more MRI services.

Working Conditions

MRI technologists work indoors within labs that contain the MRI equipment. They are often on their feet, calibrating the equipment and working with patients. They need physical strength as they may need to lift or assist patients who are moving from gurneys and wheelchairs onto the scanner table, and they might need to position body parts or pieces of equipment prior to the scan.

While some MRI technologists work typical eight-hour days, others are required to work outside normal daytime hours. This most commonly occurs at a hospital, as patients are admitted day and night. At a hospital, MRI technologists often have to work nights or weekends and might also have to be on call. Typically, new technologists are more commonly called upon to work during off hours. "New techs usually have to work their way up from nights to days," Blair says.

Earnings

In 2014, MRI technologists made an average annual salary of $67,090. Areas of greater population tend to bring in higher salaries. For example, this field was compensated best in California: San Francisco featured the highest-paid average in the nation at $102,800. Salaries also typically increase with experience. Based on 2010 survey data, an MRI tech practicing in the field typically receives incremental increases in pay during their first six to ten years of working; after this stage, they often receive greater pay increases, and by fifteen years of experience, their salaries exceed the national annual average salary of an MRI technologist.

Opportunities for Advancement

The main route for advancement as an MRI technologist is to obtain supervisory responsibilities—managing other MRI and radiography technologists and assistants. Supervisory positions include chief radiologic technologist and supervisor MRI technologist. If a technologist earns a Bachelor of Science in Radiologic Sciences, he or she has a greater chance of being promoted to a supervisory position. A bachelor's degree may also qualify an MRI technologist for a teaching position within the radiologic sciences department of a university. Going even further, if an MRI technologist earns a master's degree in health administration, he or she has a chance to obtain an administrative job, such as director of an MRI department at a hospital or diagnostic center.

What Is the Future Outlook for MRI Technologists?

The BLS projects the MRI technologist field will grow by thirty-five hundred new jobs from 2014 to 2024. This is an increase of 10 percent over current figures and is higher than the average growth rate across all jobs. This is because the population is growing older, which is often correlated with an increase in medical conditions that require MRIs for diagnosis. Additionally, with more people having health insurance, a greater number of people are able to afford MRIs. Therefore, many facilities should be able to find steady work for experienced MRI technologists.

Find Out More

American Association for Women Radiologists
1891 Preston White Dr.
Reston, VA 20191
website: www.aawr.org

This association was founded in 1981 to provide an outlet for women in radiology, radiation oncology, and related professions (such as MRI) to discuss field-related issues. The website offers information for learning more about women in the sciences and career opportunities available.

American Registry of Magnetic Resonance Imaging Technologists (ARMRIT)
2049 E. Sixty-Seventh St.
Brooklyn, NY 11234
website: www.armrit.org

ARMRIT certifies MRI technologists who have met its established criteria and requires specific MRI education, in-depth clinical training, and hands-on experience. Its website includes information on MRI schools and online courses.

American Society of Radiologic Technologists (ASRT)
5000 Central Ave. SE
Albuquerque, NM 87123
website: www.asrt.org

The ASRT is a professional association for the medical imaging and radiation therapy community. Much information is offered on its website, including journals relating to radiologic and MRI fields, career opportunities, the latest in regulations, and research.

Radiological Society of North America (RSNA)
820 Jorie Blvd.
Oak Brook, IL 60523
website: www.rsna.org

The RSNA is an international society made up of more than fifty-four thousand members from 136 countries around the world. It provides continuing education credits toward the maintenance of professional certification. The website includes several professional publications, continuing education opportunities, and the latest scientific research.

Pharmacist

What Does a Pharmacist Do?

The goal of pharmacists is to help patients get well by providing them with doctor-prescribed medications and educating them about the proper use of prescription and over-the-counter drugs. Pharmacists' duties include preparing the medications, monitoring patient response to medications, understanding potential interactions between prescriptions and other medications, and advising physicians, nurses, and insurance companies about medications and their effects. These are typical responsibilities for most pharmacists, but they might have other duties depending on the specific setting in which they work.

Community pharmacists work in a local pharmacy, which may be a stand-alone store or a pharmacy area within a larger retail chain store. These pharmacists interact with customers daily, and they often get to know their patients well. Ange, a pharmacist for more than twenty-eight years, reflected on the value of being a community pharmacist on the ValuePenguin website. She explains, "It's given me the opportunity, having worked in retail pharmacy, to

At a Glance
Pharmacist

Minimum Educational Requirements
Doctor of pharmacy (PharmD)

Personal Qualities
Detailed; attentive; ethical

Certification and Licensing
State license

Working Conditions
Indoors, in an office

Salary Range
As of 2015, the median salary was $121,500

Number of Jobs
As of 2014, about 297,100

Future Job Outlook
An increase of 3 percent through 2024

have closer relationships with my patients. And then, in turn, sometimes with their whole families. Now I'm filling scripts for people who have children now."

Typically, a community pharmacist's day begins by filling orders that have been received from physicians. The pharmacist enters the computer system to look up the intended patient and review his or her medical history. The pharmacist checks to see if the prescription will interact negatively with another drug the patient is taking or with a known medical condition. Then the pharmacist fills the prescription from the stocks within the pharmacy. When the patient arrives to pick up the medication, the pharmacist ensures that he or she understands the drug, its intended effects and potential side effects, and the instructions for proper dosage.

Some pharmacists work in hospitals and clinics. Like a community pharmacist, a clinical pharmacist dispenses refill medications and new medications to patients within the hospital or clinic. The difference between a community and a clinical pharmacist is that a clinical pharmacist spends much more time interacting with doctors and nurses who are overseeing patients in medical wards. When determining a treatment for a patient, a physician may consult with a clinical pharmacist for information about the effectiveness and potential side effects of drugs and other medicines, such as lotions and ointments. "For a professional pharmacist, it's very nice to be so close with the doctors and the nursing staff and to be able to get a hold of them when we need to," said Sara, a pharmacist, in a 2013 interview on the University of Wisconsin UWHealth website. Pharmacists in hospitals are able to update physicians on patients' reactions to prescriptions and discuss progress or continuing problems.

Another type of pharmacist is an industry pharmacist. These professionals work for drug manufacturing companies. Their jobs do not include interactions with customers. Instead, they work within the company in marketing, manufacturing, research, and product development. They provide knowledge of drugs and interactions to these areas to help the company produce and sell drugs.

Ultimately, all types of pharmacists spend much of their time keeping up to date on the latest medications, their effects, and interactions with other drugs in order to provide the best health care to patients. According to CNNMoney, pharmacist is the nineteenth-best job in the United States due to the high salary and job satisfaction. "Any time you can work with someone with a major health issue and help them get control of the disease and avoid long-term complications, that is a good day," says Justin Wilson, pharmacist in charge at Valu-Med Pharmacy in Oklahoma, on the CNNMoney website.

How Do You Become a Pharmacist?

Education

Pharmacists must obtain a doctor of pharmacy (PharmD) degree to practice. As of 2014, there were 130 graduate programs that were accredited by the Accreditation Council for Pharmacy Education to confer PharmD degrees. Many students in these programs have obtained bachelor's degrees in science-related fields. However, some programs accept applicants without bachelor's degrees if they have at least two years of undergraduate study. Whether an applicant has a degree or not, most pharmacy programs have specific post-secondary course requirements—such as chemistry, biology, and anatomy—that students must have on their transcripts. Additionally, most programs require that applicants submit scores from their Pharmacy College Admissions Test.

Once accepted to a PharmD program, students generally attend for four years, although some colleges offer a three-year program. During these programs, students study chemistry, pharmacology, and medical ethics. "My first two years I took mostly science classes, such as biochemistry, pharmacology, and medicinal chemistry," wrote Jennifer, a pharmacist, in 2016 on *Day in the Life*, a blog dedicated to inspiring teens to learn about careers. "In my third year these were replaced by courses with a therapeutic focus (therapeutic basically means we learned about different medicines and HOW we can [use] them to make people feel better when they are sick)." Additionally, during this time, students work under supervised conditions in settings like pharmacies and hospitals to obtain on-the-job experience.

After graduating from a PharmD program, pharmacists can further specialize. Those who are interested in clinical pharmacy, a research job, or specialization in an area such as geriatrics may continue by completing a one- to two-year residency at a hospital or clinic.

Certification and Licensing

A pharmacist must obtain a state license to legally work. To acquire a license, a prospective pharmacist must pass two exams. The first is the North American Pharmacist Licensure Exam, which tests specific pharmacy skills and knowledge. The second test is either the Multistate Pharmacy Jurisprudence Exam or a state-specific test, which tests applicants on their understanding of pharmacy law within a state or region. Additionally, pharmacist license applicants must complete a number of hours as interns; the requirements vary by state. Pharmacists who administer vaccinations and immunizations also need a

A pharmacist prepares a medication prescribed by a doctor. Pharmacists frequently talk with patients to make sure they know the proper way to take their medications and also are aware of possible side effects.

separate certification in most states. The majority of states typically require that these individuals complete the American Pharmacists Association's Pharmacy-Based Immunization Delivery training program for certification.

Volunteer Work and Internships

Pharmacy colleges often encourage—and some require—that applicants have either employment or volunteer experience working in a health care setting, such as a pharmacy, nursing home, hospital, or clinic. Local hospitals often have volunteer positions available that students can apply for as an undergraduate or high school student. Additionally, national organizations, such as the Red Cross, can provide information on volunteer opportunities in health fields in local areas.

Skills and Personality

An essential skill of pharmacists is the ability to pay attention to detail. Pharmacists label and dispense potentially dangerous medications, and they need to ensure that they provide their patients with the correct medication, dosage, and instructions. Additionally, pharmacists must keep detailed records of patients' prescriptions, so this skill comes in handy in other parts of the job.

Pharmacists should also be ethical, as they are trusted by law to handle dangerous and potentially habit-forming substances. If these substances got into the wrong hands, they could cause major health problems and even death. A good pharmacist stringently follows the law when it comes to dispensing pharmaceuticals.

Being able to communicate well is necessary for a pharmacist because most pharmacists spend time interacting with patients. A pharmacist must be able to give clear instructions to patients and listen carefully to their questions and concerns. Clinical pharmacist Matthew Bledsoe said, "I enjoy the one-on-one conversations I have with patients in their rooms on a daily basis, not only the talks about medications but the important debates like 'Krispy Kreme' or 'Dunkin Donuts,'" in a 2011 article for the website Pharmacy Times. Additionally, pharmacists deal with doctors and insurance companies on a daily basis, requiring the ability to clearly express themselves.

On the Job

Employers

Pharmacists generally work in hospitals, clinics, and retail pharmacies. Of these, retail pharmacies employ the greatest numbers; according to the Bureau of Labor Statistics (BLS), 42 percent of pharmacists work in this setting. Additionally, 19 percent of pharmacists work in medical and surgical hospitals. A smaller number of pharmacists are employed in research labs at pharmaceutical companies.

Working Conditions

Pharmacists mainly work indoors at pharmacies. They are often on their feet, as they fill prescriptions and interact with people while filling prescriptions. The majority of pharmacists work full time, but one in five worked part time in 2014, according to the Department of Labor. Most full-time pharmacists work a forty-hour workweek, but as some pharmacies are open all hours, pharmacists may end up working nights or weekends.

Earnings

Pharmacists are paid well. According to the BLS, in 2015, the average salary of a pharmacist was $119,270. The lowest 10 percent earned less than $86,790 per year, and the highest 10 percent earned more than $154,040. The highest-paid pharmacists are employed by scientific research and development companies. Additionally, location affects pharmacist salaries; those in metropolitan areas, such as Santa Cruz, California; Gadsden, Alabama; and Fresno, California, are on the upper end of the scale.

Opportunities for Advancement

Different advancement options are available to pharmacists. For one, they can aspire to open their own pharmacies. In this case, a business background via classes or self-study is necessary in order to run the business. Additionally, they will often need to work longer hours in order to ensure that both the pharmaceutical and business sides of their pharmacy are in order.

Those who work in a medical facility, such as a hospital, have a variety of advancement options. There are also management tracks within hospitals that allow pharmacists to become head pharmacists. These individuals are in charge of training interns and managing other pharmacists and pharmacist assistants.

Pharmacists working for pharmaceutical companies can also follow a management track. They can work toward leadership positions within their departments or toward becoming a department head.

What Is the Future Outlook for Pharmacists?

In 2014, according to the BLS, there were 297,100 pharmacists in the United States. The projected increase by 2024 is ninety-one hundred jobs, or a job growth of about 3 percent. This is lower than the average growth rate for all occupations. Opposing factors affect the future job growth for pharmacists. On the one hand, a growing population of elderly people requires more prescription medicines than young people do. Additionally, rates of chronic diseases treated with prescription medications are rising. These factors lead to an increased need of pharmacists. On the other hand, more people are ordering their prescriptions online, which reduces the need for pharmacists in local retail stores, where most are employed.

Find Out More

American Association of Colleges of Pharmacy (AACP)
1727 King St.
Alexandria, VA 22314
website: www.aacp.org

The AACP is an association that provides members the opportunity to take professional development programs and access publications with the latest professional information. Its website offers people an opportunity to search for pharmaceutical schools. It also includes links to journals providing the latest research on drugs and treatments.

American Pharmacists Association (APA)
2215 Constitution Ave. NW
Washington, DC 20037
website: www.pharmacist.com

The APA is the largest association of pharmacists in the United States. Its more than sixty-two thousand members receive free online learning courses and ways to connect with other pharmacists. The organization's website provides information on the latest health updates, pharmacist jobs available, and online training programs.

American Society of Health-System Pharmacists (ASHP)
7272 Wisconsin Ave.
Bethesda, MD 20814
website: www.ashp.org

The ASHP represents pharmacists who serve as patient care providers in acute and ambulatory settings. It provides pharmacists with the latest information on drug therapies. Its website provides a way for pharmacists to search for jobs across the country and online information about the latest drugs.

National Community Pharmacists Association (NCPA)
100 Daingerfield Rd.
Alexandria, VA 22314
website: www.ncpanet.org

The NCPA consists of America's community pharmacists. Its mission is to provide support for community pharmacists by keeping up with the latest pharmaceutical laws and regulations. Its website includes up-to-date actions in Washington, DC, on issues of health care and an online link to *America's Pharmacist*, a magazine with the latest pharmaceutical news.

Pediatrician

What Does a Pediatrician Do?

One of the biggest decisions parents expecting a newborn make is whom to choose for their child's pediatrician. A pediatrician is an integral part of a child's life from infancy to young adulthood. Pediatricians oversee the physical, mental, and emotional health of children. A general pediatrician diagnoses and treats illnesses and injuries, conducts wellness exams to assess a child's health, determines necessary vaccinations, and provides information to both the child and parents about health, safety, fitness, and nutrition needs. Most pediatricians work either in private practices or on staff at hospitals.

On an average day, a pediatrician at a hospital will go on rounds. During this time, the pediatrician visits various wards with young patients, such as the newborn nursery and pediatric ward. There, the pediatrician will take vitals and check each patient's status; assess if any treatment is needed and, if so, determine what the treatment should be; and visit with parents to communicate the child's health status. Robert Stone, who

At a Glance
Pediatrician

Minimum Educational Requirements
Doctor of medicine (MD)

Personal Qualities
Analytical; observant; empathetic

Certification and Licensing
Certification from American Board of Pediatrics; state license

Working Conditions
Indoors, in an office

Salary Range
As of 2015, the median salary was $171,300

Number of Jobs
As of May 2015, about 28,660

Future Job Outlook
An increase of 10 percent through 2024

was named the 2002 Pediatrician of the Year by the Ohio chapter of the American Academy of Pediatrics, explained in 2013 to the Akron Children's Hospital online newsletter that a pediatrician needs to be attentive to not just the physical, but also the emotional needs of patients and their parents. "You may go into one exam room to see a new baby and really be able to help the parents deal with their anxieties with a sense of humor," Stone said. "The next room may have a very ill child or a teenager who is anxious about school, personal inter-relationships." After two or three hours of rounds, the pediatrician returns to his or her private office at the hospital to begin patient appointments in which he or she assesses wellness of patients and diagnoses and treats health issues.

Pediatricians who work in private practices experience a similar day, except instead of rounds, they attend scheduled appointments with their patients at their office. These appointments include making wellness checks, attending to sickness or injury complaints, providing preventive care, diagnosing and determining treatment, and providing overall health advice. At the end of the day, when appointments are done, pediatricians in both private practices and hospitals still must see to paperwork, lab results, X-rays, and prescription refill requests. When these are completed, a pediatrician's day is finally over—unless he or she is called in after hours with an emergency.

Pediatricians who have obtained a subspecialty deal with more specific children's health issues. The Council of Pediatric Subspecialties lists twenty different subspecialties that pediatricians may choose to pursue after pediatric residency. For example, a pediatric neonatologist specializes in treating critically ill infants. A pediatric hematologist/oncologist diagnoses and treats children with cancer and a variety of different blood disorders. Often pediatric subspecialists work in hospitals, assessing and providing patient care there in their specialties.

No matter what area a pediatrician chooses, studies show that the majority seem satisfied with their careers. While pediatricians are among the lower paid of medical doctors, they are still well compensated and are happy with the balance of their work hours and their home life. For reasons such as this, *U.S. News & World Report* ranked the job of pediatrician number eight on their 2016 list of 100 Best Jobs.

How Do You Become a Pediatrician?

Education

Becoming a pediatrician is an intensive endeavor, requiring many years of schooling. Preparation begins in high school, where students should ideally take chemistry, biology, physics, calculus, and other mathematics and science classes to prepare them for college. A bachelor's degree is the first requirement of a pediatrician. A bachelor's degree in a premedical field—such as biology—is helpful but not required in order to be accepted to an accredited medical school.

Medical schools do require several prerequisite courses in math and science—such as biology, chemistry, and calculus—in order to be accepted. Additionally, medical school applicants need to score high on the Medical College Admissions Test to obtain admittance. Medical school takes four years to complete. During the first two years, students learn basic medical sciences, such as human anatomy, physiology, chemistry, microbiology, pharmacology, and neuroanatomy. The second two years of medical school are when students learn clinical sciences, which is when they get hands-on experience with patients.

Following medical school, aspiring pediatricians enter an accredited pediatric residency for three years. At this point, they are officially doctors but are not fully trained. During their residency, new doctors learn how to diagnose and treat children while working long, intense hours alongside more experienced doctors. Following residency, general pediatricians have completed their education, but if they are interested in a subspecialty, such as cardiology or hematology, this generally requires another three years of study.

Certification and Licensing

All physicians in the United States must meet their states' requirements to receive a license to practice. All states require that an applicant has graduated from an accredited medical school and is able to pass the US Medical Licensing Examination to become a doctor of medicine or the Comprehensive Osteopathic Medical Licensing

Examination to become a doctor of osteopathic medicine. Additionally, after pediatricians complete a residency program, they must pass the American Board of Pediatrics board-certified pediatrician exam in order to qualify for a state license in their field.

Volunteer Work and Internships

For a student interested in becoming a pediatrician, volunteering at a local hospital, clinic, or other health care establishment can provide a way to learn about health care settings and to observe people working in the industry. In a National Association for College Admission Counseling seminar on medical school admissions, presenters suggested that exposure to the medical profession with practical experience in a doctor's office, clinic, or hospital are all beneficial ways to discover if a student is truly interested in medicine.

For college students, there are research and medical internships available during summers at select universities. Typically, those with premed or scientific majors, such as biology, can apply for these. Certain hospitals, such as Children's Hospital in Los Angeles, also offer internships for high school students who like to work with children. These are usually volunteer programs that entail reading to patients and assisting in playrooms. Other hospitals throughout the country offer similar types of internships and volunteer positions.

Skills and Personality

An interest in sciences and an analytical mind are necessary to pediatricians because they must assess their patients' health and diagnose health problems. This can be challenging considering that young patients are often scared or not always capable of explaining themselves well. Pediatricians need to be active listeners, good observers, and resourceful thinkers as they study their patients. They listen and look for both obvious and subtle changes in a patient's health and then use the resources available, such as therapies and drugs, to determine the best method of treatment. Additionally, they often possess an interest in continual learning in order to keep abreast of the latest medical techniques and information.

Personality traits, such as being a good communicator and showing empathy, help pediatricians as they interact with young patients and their parents. Compassion is also essential, as pediatricians must provide not only medical support but also emotional support to patients undergoing chronic medical problems. Steve Abrams, neonatologist and professor of pediatrics at the University of Texas Dell Medical School, says in *U.S. News & World Report*, "Sometimes you have to give really bad news to families. Not all of medicine is about making people well."

Enjoying children is also a must. Abrams explains that this is one of the many joys of his job. "It's one of the few jobs where a doctor gets to hug his patients," he states. Often pediatricians know their patients for years, seeing them from infants until young adulthood, and establish connections with them.

On the Job

Employers

The majority of pediatricians work in traditional doctors' offices where patients, whether sick or well, receive care. Pediatricians who have specialized in an area, such as oncology, usually work in hospitals within their fields. Pediatricians also may work in academic institutions, universities, medical schools, and teaching hospitals, where they teach and train others about medicine and pediatrics. Additionally, some pediatricians work as researchers who conduct studies and trials to move pediatric medicine forward. Research pediatricians typically work for professional organizations, such as the American Academy of Pediatrics' research department, or within universities' medical programs or in hospitals.

Working Conditions

Pediatricians typically work at a private practice or at a hospital. They are on their feet most of the day, tending to the children in their care. Most work relatively normal hours. The 2014 Medscape Pediatrician Compensation Report found 43 percent of respondents to a pediatrician survey reported that they worked thirty to forty hours a week seeing patients, and one-third of the respondents reported seeing twenty-five to seventy-five patients each week. Additionally, they may work after hours because of patient emergencies. If a patient has a serious problem after hours, pediatricians may either be called to consult with them or, if it is an emergency, may need to meet their patients at a hospital. Pediatricians in hospitals work more demanding schedules with on-call hours, but they may have more flexibility than a typical nine-to-five schedule.

Earnings

Pediatricians tend to make less money than doctors who specialize in other fields. Medscape's 2014 Compensation Report stated that pediatricians' salaries are third from the bottom among all physicians. However, pediatricians still earn high salaries compared to most jobs. According to the Bureau of Labor Statistics (BLS), the annual average salary for pediatricians in 2015 was $183,180. Those who work in private practices generally are on the higher end of the scale, with an average of $188,420. Salaries vary based on location, years of experience, and where the pediatrician works, such as in a hospital, research facility, academic institution, or private practice.

Opportunities for Advancement

A pediatrician working in a hospital can advance by becoming the head of a department or division where he or she will manage other pediatricians, nurses, and medical staff. For example, in a division within a hospital, such as pediatric surgery, a person can work at becoming the chief pediatric surgeon who leads a group of pediatric surgeons. Those working in research facilities can also advance to the position of lead researcher in a field of study.

What Is the Future Outlook for Pediatricians?

The BLS projects a 10 percent increase in pediatricians from 2014 to 2024, from a base of 34,800 pediatricians working in 2014. This increase is above the average projected growth for all occupations. Pediatricians willing to work in rural or low-income areas have the greatest employment opportunities because these areas typically lack adequate numbers of doctors. One reason for the projected growth is that health care reform laws have increased insurance coverage and access for children to medical care. Additionally, there have been an increasing number of children who deal with significant chronic health problems. According to the American Academy of Pediatrics, about ten to twenty million children and adolescents in the United States have some form of chronic illness or disability, such as anemia or diabetes, leading to a need for more pediatric care.

Find Out More

Academic Pediatrician Association (APA)
6728 Old McLean Village Dr.
McLean, VA 22101
website: http://academicpeds.org

The APA works to improve the overall health of children and adolescents through research, education, and developing health care delivery methods. The website includes publications with the latest developments of the APA in policies, research, and health care delivery.

American Academy of Pediatrics (AAP)
141 Northwest Point Blvd.
Elk Grove Village, IL 60007
website: www.aap.com

The AAP's goal is to obtain optimal physical, mental, and social health and well-being for all US infants, children, adolescents, and young adults. It is a professional membership consisting of more than sixty-six thousand pediatricians. On its website, the AAP provides pediatricians with information concerning the latest research and health practices.

American Board of Pediatrics (ABP)
111 Silver Cedar Ct.
Chapel Hill, NC 27514
website: www.abp.org

The ABP is one of the American Board of Medical Specialties' certifying boards. The ABP is an independent nonprofit organization that certifies general pediatricians and pediatricians with subspecialties. Visitors to the organization's website can find specific information regarding the boards and testing.

Council of Pediatric Subspecialties (CoPS)
6728 Old McLean Village Dr.
McLean, VA 22101

website: www.pedsubs.org

This organization provides information on its website regarding the various pediatric subspecialties, what career opportunities are available within these subspecialties, and how to obtain a subspecialty. CoPS works to ensure subspecialties are working together and communicating to further children's health.

Occupational Therapist

What Does an Occupational Therapist Do?

Occupational therapists (OTs) work with individuals who have conditions that are mentally, physically, developmentally, or emotionally disabling. An occupational therapist's goal is to enable these people to accomplish the daily tasks of life, such as eating and bathing. They use skills and knowledge from several disciplines to help teach their clients how to improve or regain mental and bodily functions. For example, they will help a patient overcoming hip replacement surgery learn to use a walker with a gait belt to increase mobility. Others might teach a child with ADHD to use specific sensory stimulation to learn to relax and stay attentive, allowing the child to accomplish schoolwork.

Occupational therapists most often work in hospitals, schools, rehabilitation centers, and home care agencies. In all of these settings, the

At a Glance

Occupational Therapist

Minimum Educational Requirements

Master's degree

Personal Qualities

Cooperative; empathetic; organized

Certification and Licensing

State license required

Working Conditions

Indoors, in a room with equipment; some lifting required

Salary Range

As of 2015, the median salary was $80,150

Number of Jobs

As of 2014, about 114,600

Future Job Outlook

An increase of 27 percent through 2024

duties of an occupational therapist are similar, but the types of patient conditions are often different. On a typical day, an occupational therapist meets with both new and regular patients who have been prescribed occupational therapy by a physician. When meeting with a new patient, the occupational therapist does an initial assessment by reviewing the patient's medical history, asking the patient questions, and observing the patient performing tasks. Then, the occupational therapist evaluates the patient's condition and needs and develops a treatment plan for the patient. This plan identifies specific goals and the types of activities that will be used to help the patient work toward those goals.

Specifically, the goals are related to accomplishing life tasks. Over time, the occupational therapist will meet with the patient, perform exercises and tasks with the patient, assign the patient exercises to perform in between appointments, and track his or her progress toward their ability to function with everyday tasks. For example, a stroke victim may have limited mobility with his or her hands, and while a physical therapist will work with the patient to increase strength and dexterity of the hands, an occupational therapist will focus on exercise and methods that will teach the patient how to get dressed or eat meals on his or her own.

When creating plans for their patients, occupational therapists determine both short-term and long-term goals. Kashala Erby, an occupational therapist who works at a nursing home, created a plan for a stroke patient based on the goals they determined together. The long-term goal for the patient was to improve his upper body strength so that he could dress independently and later push his wheelchair to the dining room. Erby developed several short-term goals that he could work toward during the process. "The treatment process begins by teaching him how to roll his wheelchair to the OT gym using both the left and right side of his body," she explained in a 2013 *Minority Nurse* online article. "If his left side was too weak, I would teach him a one-sided technique." Erby continued to work with her patient, helping him progress toward these goals.

While occupational therapists spend most of their time working with patients, they must also complete administrative work. They document their patient plans, progress, and any problems encountered. These reports are used by others who work with the patient, such as physical therapists or physicians, to monitor patient progress and condition. At the end of the day, occupational therapists look over their upcoming schedule and review the files of patients they will see the next day.

For those who are interested in working directly with people while using scientific knowledge—such as understanding how sensory processing can affect a person's ability to focus, and understanding the role of the brain in controlling human movement—occupational therapy is a career to consider. With a high projected growth rate, those who choose to become occupational therapists will likely discover a stable and interesting career.

How Do You Become an Occupational Therapist?

Education

In order to practice, occupational therapists must possess a master's degree in occupational therapy from an accredited program. In 2014 there were nearly two hundred occupational therapy programs in the United States accredited by the Accreditation Council for Occupational Therapy Education. To be admitted to a graduate program, an applicant needs a bachelor's degree, along with specific class credits, including biology and physiology. Typically, master's programs take two to three years to complete. There are some schools that offer a dual-degree occupational therapy program in which the student earns a bachelor's degree and a master's degree over the course of five years. Whatever program they choose, students learn about anatomy, patient care, and assistive technology in their field. As part of the program, students will perform twenty-four weeks of supervised clinical fieldwork. This fieldwork can take place in nursing homes, rehabilitation centers, schools, or even private practices.

Certification and Licensing

All states require occupational therapists to be licensed. Although licensing requirements vary by state, every candidate must pass the national examination administered by the National Board for Certification in Occupational Therapy (NBCOT). All candidates must have earned a degree from an accredited occupational therapist program and have completed all fieldwork requirements before taking the exam. Therapists who pass the NBCOT exam may use the title occupational therapist, registered in whatever position they later acquire.

Volunteer Work and Internships

Prior to deciding whether or not to follow an occupational therapist career, volunteering in a hospital, nursing home, or similar facility can provide prospective students with experience working with patients in a health care setting. For students who want to get hands-on experience—and graduates who want to build on their experience— there are several OT internships available both in the United States and around the world. These internships are typically volunteer positions. For example, Projects Abroad offers volunteer internships around the world for various professionals, including occupational therapists.

Skills and Personality

Being a good communicator is necessary for occupational therapists because they must listen carefully to their patients in order to understand what their goals are. Then, therapists need to be able to clearly explain and demonstrate to patients how to perform certain exercises. Finally, they must be able to assess any problems or concerns patients have by carefully listening to questions and complaints.

Being a team player will also help occupational therapists perform their job successfully. Throughout their day, they interact not only with patients but also with their patients' families. The ability to include family in their patients' exercises and work will help patients progress toward their goals. In addition to patients and their families, occupational therapists work with physicians, nurses, physical therapists, and speech therapists who are involved in their patients' recovery. Collaborating with these medical professionals is beneficial to determining the best paths toward improvement.

Furthermore, organizational skills are a must for occupational therapists because they create plans for their patients, track their patients' progress, ensure they meet with their patients on schedule, and complete necessary paperwork. With this skill, however, comes a need to be flexible when dealing with changing situations and patient responses. This is especially true when dealing with children, notes Jordan Farver, an occupational therapist at Akron Children's Hospital. "While you always need to be prepared and have a plan, with children you need to over plan," explained Farver in a 2013 article on the hospital's website. "You never know what's going to work, and you have to be ready to rethink your plan at any time."

On the Job

Employers

Occupational therapists work for a variety of health care organizations, such as hospitals, community mental health centers, nursing homes, schools, outpatient clinics, rehabilitation centers, day care centers, research centers, and private health agencies. Some are even employed in the Peace Corps and in the military. Typically, the type of facility or assignment determines the kinds of afflictions that occupational therapists are likely to see. An occupational therapist working in a nursing home will commonly handle stroke victims and those who are recovering from hip or knee surgery, while a school occupational therapist may deal with children who have autism and those with learning disabilities.

The greatest number of occupational therapists, 27 percent according to the Bureau of Labor Statistics (BLS), work in hospitals. This can be an exciting and stressful place to work as the types of patient challenges are always changing. "The need to always be on top of your information, and the pace that is required to provide quality patient care keeps me interested and also keeps things from becoming too routine or mundane," explained Caleb Templeton, an OT with eight years of experience, in a 2016 interview on the website OT Potential.

Working Conditions

Being an occupational therapist can be physically tiring. Therapists often spend a lot of time standing and walking while working with patients. At times, they need to lift and move patients or heavy equipment in order to help their patients perform required exercises.

Occupational therapists must deal with bodily fluids when working with patients. Patients, particularly ones who have recently undergone surgery, can become nauseous during therapy, and the therapists must clean up after them if they are sick. Also, if occupational therapists are working with those recovering from surgery or an injury, they may need to deal with wound care, which involves wound packing—cleaning discharge from wounds that are infected—during therapy sessions. Dealing with these requires special attention and care to ensure they do not expose themselves to biological hazards. Those who deal with wounds must take a special course first.

Occupational therapists work indoors, in offices or rooms with specialized equipment. Many work in multiple facilities and must travel from one job to another, as well as to clients' homes. Most work full time, but in 2014 approximately 25 percent worked part-time schedules. The hours they work may vary, as occupational therapists usually must accommodate their patients' schedules.

Earnings

According to the BLS, the median annual salary for occupational therapists was $80,150 in 2015. The highest-paid 10 percent in the profession made more than $116,030 per year, while the bottom 10 percent made less than $53,250. People in metropolitan areas, such as Las Vegas; Beaumont, Texas; and Daytona Beach, Florida, receive the higher end of the pay scale. Also, occupational therapists who worked for nursing homes received above the median; while those employed by schools received below the median.

Opportunities for Advancement

For an occupational therapist, becoming a supervisor of other therapists or becoming a manager of occupational therapy within a therapy clinic are ways to advance. Occupational therapists can also choose to further their education by obtaining a PhD in occupational therapy, and this can open up more paths to advancement, such as becoming a director of a therapy program, or becoming a director or dean at a college that offers occupational therapy degrees.

What Is the Future Outlook for Occupational Therapists?

The growth outlook for occupational therapist jobs is much greater than average, with a projected 27 percent growth between 2014 and 2024, according to the BLS. Because there is an expanding aging population, studies indicate that many of these people are working to maintain their physical health and independence as they grow older. Occupational therapists are needed to help these people deal with any physical issues that inhibit their ability to live on their own. In addition, an increased number of younger patients diagnosed with autism—which was once overlooked and often undiagnosed—is fueling the need for more occupational therapists. More therapists will be needed in schools to assist these children with improving their ability to accomplish everyday tasks.

Find Out More

American Occupational Therapy Association (AOTA)
4720 Montgomery Ln.
Bethesda, MD 20824
website: www.aota.org

AOTA provides information about occupational therapy for both therapists and patients. The website gives specifics on how to become an occupational therapist and obtain a license. It also provides information on continuing education and certification in specialty areas.

American Occupational Therapy Foundation (AOTF)
4720 Montgomery Ln., Suite 202
Bethesda, MD 20814
website: www.aotf.org

The AOTF, founded in 1965, is a charitable organization that supports occupational therapy research through grants and scholarships, research programs, and publications. The website provides information to students on applying for scholarships and grants for research.

National Board for Certification in Occupational Therapy (NBCOT)
12 S. Summit Ave., Suite 100
Gaithersburg, MD 20877
website: www.nbcot.org

The NBCOT develops and provides a standard for certification of occupational therapy practitioners. The organization develops and administers the certification process. On the website, visitors can learn about the certification process, review information on how to become certified, and find online practice and study guides.

World Federation of Occupational Therapists (WFOT)
PO Box 30
Forrestfield
Western Australia
Australia 6058
website: www.wfot.org

The WFOT is a nonprofit organization that promotes occupational therapy worldwide. The website provides educational opportunities for occupational therapy around the world. Also on the website is the *WFOT Bulletin*, the official publication of the WFOT.

Interview with a Chiropractor

Maria Funicello first attended nursing school before deciding to change careers and become a chiropractor. She obtained her chiropractic degree twenty years ago from Palmer College of Chiropractic West in San Jose, California. She eventually decided to open her own practice in Scottsdale, Arizona. Funicello answered questions about her career by e-mail.

Q: Why did you become a chiropractor?

A: I decided to become a chiropractor because I wanted to help people to feel better, and to be a part of wellness. Chiropractic practices allow people's bodies to be corrected so that the body can function better on its own. I went to nursing school, prior to deciding to become a chiropractor, and quickly realized that medicine is working with sickness. I changed my path because instead, I wanted to be involved with wellness, which is what chiropractic practice allows me to do.

Q: Can you describe your typical workday?

A: I own my own practice, so I work a schedule that best fits my lifestyle. Most chiropractors are self-employed, but times are changing and other integrative practices are bringing chiropractic into the primary care facilities. However, I am able to maintain my own practice, and maintain flexibility. For right now, I am working part time, and see my patients during set appointments that I make with them. At my appointments, I spend about fifteen to thirty minutes adjusting my patients, and educating them about what I am doing and why, while making good relationships with them.

Q: What do you like most and least about your job?

A: I love my job because chiropractic practice helps my patients get out of their pain and stay comfortable in their bodies. What I like least about this career is that it is challenging to deal with insurance companies in order to get compensated for our value. Another issue is that certain medical doctors are threatened by our value.

Q: What were the most interesting and the hardest parts of chiropractor school?

A: To me, I thought the most interesting part about chiropractic school was the content itself, and that the curriculum is slightly different dependent upon the state. This was 20 years ago, so today it is likely some of [the] curriculum and courses have changed. The hardest part of attending chiropractic school was the constant studying and diligence to work. Additionally, the National Board tests were difficult, but luckily I went to a school that prepared us well for the exams. Taking the exams was probably more nerve-wracking than anything else.

Q: What personal qualities do you find most valuable for this type of work?

A: In order to become a chiropractor, people must have the strong desire to help people. They also must be self-motivated, and have the desire to be creative both building and maintaining a business.

Q: What do you see changing in your field in the future?

A: I am hoping that eventually chiropractic practices will be included into primary care for patients. I believe that different disciplines of doctors working together would be a positive aspect focusing on the good of the patient.

Q: What advice do you have for students who might be interested in this career?

A: My best advice is for aspiring chiropractors to do their homework on what is available for chiropractors. Investigate the different career paths there are for chiropractors. Everything is changing in the world of health care, so don't be afraid to think out of the box and be creative!

Other Careers in Medicine

Anesthesiologist
Cardiologist
Cardiovascular Technologist
Clinical Laboratory Technician
Dental Hygienist
Diagnostic Medical
    Sonographer
Emergency Medical Technician
Family Practitioner
Home Health Aide
Licensed Practical Nurse
Massage Therapist
Medical Assistant
Nurse Anesthetist
Nurse Midwife
Obstetrician
Occupational Therapy Assistant
Ophthalmologist

Optician
Optometrist
Pharmacy Technician
Phlebotomist
Physical Therapist
Physical Therapy Assistant
Physician
Physician Assistant
Podiatrist
Psychiatrist
Psychologist
Radiologic Technologist
Registered Nurse
Respiratory Therapist
Speech-Language Pathologist
Surgeon
Surgical Technologist

Editor's Note: The US Department of Labor's Bureau of Labor Statistics provides information about hundreds of occupations. The agency's *Occupational Outlook Handbook* describes what these jobs entail, the work environment, education and skill requirements, pay, future outlook, and more. The *Occupational Outlook Handbook* may be accessed online at www.bls.gov/ooh.

Index

Picture Credits

About the Author

Leanne Currie-McGhee lives in Norfolk, Virginia, with her husband, two girls (Grace and Hope), and their dog, Delilah. She has been writing educational books for over a decade.